The

ENDLESS BANQUET

A Thematic Explanation of the Qur'an

VOLUME ONE

By
HAMZAH ABDUL-MALIK

Imam Ghazali PUBLISHING

© Imam Ghazali Publishing, New Jersey, USA

ISBN: 978-1-952306-46-4

No part of this publication may be reproduced, stored in a retrieval system, or transmitted in any form or by any means, electronic or otherwise, including photocopying, recording, and internet without prior permission of Imam Ghazali Publishing.

Title	The Endless Banquet: A Thematic Explanation of the Qur'an (Volume One)
Author	Hamzah Abdul-Malik
Proofreader	www.igpconsultants.com | info@igpconsultants.com
Book Design	www.igpconsultants.com | info@igpconsultants.com
Distribution	www.sattaurpublishing.com | info@sattaurpublishing.com

All rights reserved. Aside from fair use, meaning a few pages or less for non-profit educational purposes, review, or scholarly citation, no part of this publication may be reproduced, stored in a retrieval system, or transmitted in any form or by any means, electronic, mechanical, photocopying, recording, or otherwise, without the prior permission of the Copyright owner.

info@imamghazalipublishing.com
www.imamghazalipublishing.com

Bulk Ordering Information: Special discounts are available on quantity purchases. For details, please contact the publishers.

Proudly printed in the USA.

The views, information, or opinions expressed are solely those of the author(s) and do not necessarily represent those of the publisher.

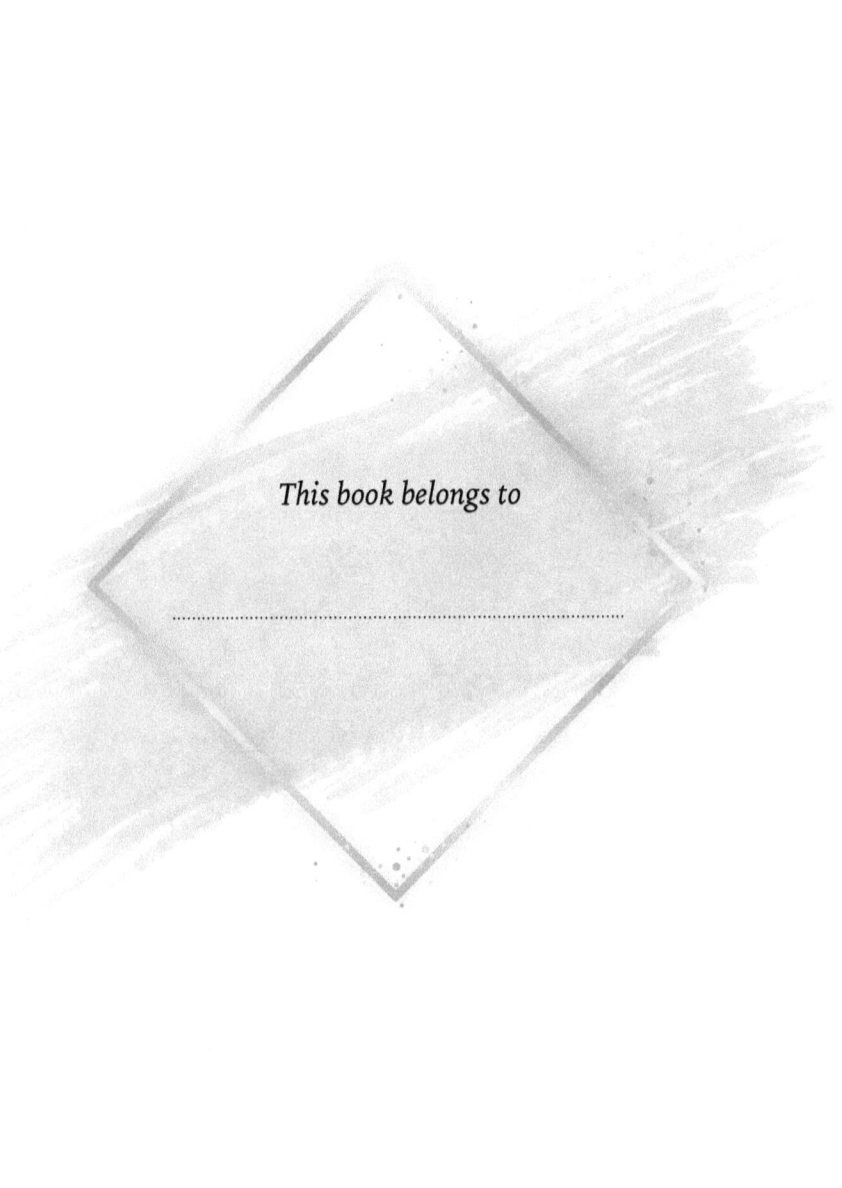

All praise belongs to Allah who revealed the Qur'an and made it a light that illuminates the hearts of every believing woman and man. May He send the most sublime salutation of peace and blessings upon the most beloved of all creation, and upon his family and companions until the Day of Intercession.

CONTENTS

	Author's Introduction	XI
Juz 1 **The Human Condition**	**Surah al-Fātiḥah**	3
	Surah al-Baqarah	4
	Āyāt 1-20	4
	Āyāt 21-29	5
	Āyāt 30-39	5
	Āyāt 40-50	5
	Āyāt 51-66	6
	Āyāt 67-80	6
	Āyāt 81- 93	7
	Āyāt 94-101	7
	Āyāt 95-123	7
	Āyāt 124-141	9
Juz 2 **The New Covenant**	Āyāt 142-162	13
	Āyāt 163-176	14
	Āyāt 177-203	14
	Āyāt 204-222	15
	Āyāt 223-242	16
	Āyāt 243-252	16
Juz 3 **The Power of Allah**	Āyāt 253-260	21
	Āyāt 261-262	22
	Āyāt 263-274	22
	Āyāt 275-283	23
	Āyāt 284-286	24
	Surah āl ʿImrān	25
	Āyāt 1-9	25
	Āyāt 10-22	27
	Āyāt 23-32	27
	Āyāt 33-63	28
	Āyāt 64-83	28
	Āyāt 84-91	29

Juz 4
Protecting the Community

Āyāt 92-99	33
Āyāt 100-120	33
Āyāt 121-148	34
Āyāt 149-172	35
Āyāt 171-180	36
Āyāt 181-200	37

Surah al-Nisā' — **38**

Āyāt 1-14	38

Juz 5
Social Reform

Āyāt 24-32	43
Āyāt 33-57	43
Āyāt 58-70	44
Āyāt 71-86	44
Āyāt 87-94	45
Āyāt 95-104	47
Āyāt 105-126	47
Āyāt 127-130	48
Āyāt 131-147	48

Juz 6
Upholding the Religion

Āyāt 148-161	53
Āyāt 162-176	53

Surah al-Mā'idah — **54**

Āyāt 1-5	54
Āyāt 6-16	55
Āyāt 17-26	55
Āyāt 27-40	56
Āyāt 41-57	56
Āyāt 58-71	57
Āyāt 72-81	58

Juz 7
The Transcendence of Allah

Āyāt 82-91	63
Āyāt 92-108	63
Āyāt 109-120	64

Surah al-An'ām — **64**

Āyāt 1-19	64

Āyāt 20-35	65
Āyāt 36-58	67
Āyāt 59-72	67
Āyāt 73-90	68
Āyāt 91-94	68
Āyāt 95-111	69

Juz 8 — History Repeats

Āyāt 112-132	73
Āyāt 133-147	74
Āyāt 148-153	74
Āyāt 154-165	75

Surah al-Aʻrāf — **76**

Āyāt 1-10	76
Āyāt 11-20	76
Āyāt 21-42	77
Āyāt 43-56	78
Āyāt 57-87	78

Juz 9 — True Liberation

Āyāt 88-102	85
Āyāt 103-131	85
Āyāt 132-137	86
Āyāt 138-155	87
Āyāt 156-178	88
Āyāt 179-206	89

Surah al-Anfāl — **90**

Āyāt 1- 19	90
Āyāt 20-40	91

Juz 10 — Hypocrisy

Āyāt 41-54	95
Āyāt 55-66	95
Āyāt 67-75	97

Surah al-Tawbah — **98**

Āyāt 1-15	98
Āyāt 16-37	98
Āyāt 38-66	100
Āyāt 67-74	101
Āyāt 75-92	101

AUTHOR'S INTRODUCTION

> We have made the Qur'an easy to understand, but is there anyone who would pay attention? [54:17]

I was 10 years old when I was first asked to read through the whole Qur'an in English. I had memorized almost half of the Qur'an by then, so I was excited to begin learning what it all meant. However, I distinctly remember opening up a Yusuf Ali translation and reading words like "thou", "thy", "similitude", and "hath not". As a child, I felt as if I needed to take a class in Shakespearian language before being able to know what the Qur'an means. I was able to finish reading the translation during Ramadan, but it was difficult.

As I grew older, I dedicated myself to learning Arabic. I finished memorizing the Qur'an, spent 15 years studying overseas, and eventually graduated from al-Azhar University. During that time, I began coming across translations that were easier to read. Yet, I still felt there was something lost: I couldn't see the connections between the āyāt and Surahs by reading the translations alone. At that time, if you asked me what the relationship was between Surah al-Baqarah and Surah Āl 'Imrān, I would have had no idea. I wouldn't have even been able to describe the connections between the beginning and end of any given Surah.

All this changed when I became connected to two scholars: Habīb 'Umar b. Hāfidh and Imam Muhammad Mutawallī al-Shaʿrāwī. I used to attend Habīb 'Umar's public tafsīr lectures in the city square in Tarim, where he would weave the Qur'anic themes together and explain it as if Allah was speaking directly to us. Then I moved to Egypt and began - and ultimately completed - translating over 1,500 pages of Imam al-Shaʿrāwī's commentary of Surah *al-Mā'idah* and *al-Tawba*. This process opened my eyes to the wholistic messages of the Qur'an and the undercurrent of themes that connect the Qur'an to our everyday lives. I began thinking, "If people who know Arabic have difficulty understanding these connections on their own, then it must be even harder for those who don't know Arabic." I began looking for a reading guide that could help the average person understand broader meanings of the Qur'an in the translation they were reading and develop a greater appreciation for what Allah was saying. And it is for that reason why I began writing this book, which was completed on the 27th of Ramadan 1441/2020.

The Endless Banquet is a reading guide of the Qur'an for people who want to have an intimate relationship with the Qur'an and read it as if Allah is speaking directly to them. It was written in easy language and focuses on explaining each Surah by grouping its āyāt together that share common themes. If you want to read the Qur'an and study its fundamental themes and connections without having to resort to sorting through thousands of pages of Arabic tafsīr, then this book is designed for you.

Throughout the book you will discover the benefits of why certain phrases are repeated, why the Qur'an repeats the same stories but with different details, the wisdom of how āyāt shift from speaking about law to stories, or from theological arguments to descriptions of heaven and hell. You can discover connections between each Surah of the Qur'an and see the wisdom in their order and even learn how each Juz is divided upon overarching themes. This book will teach you the context for why certain āyāt are revealed and why they are still relevant today.

Ultimately, the goal of this book is to help people develop an appreciation for the Qur'an, especially the parts of the Qur'an that they don't usually read. By using this guide, they can begin developing a greater sense of wonder and awe that the Qur'an is supposed to inspire in the reader. Ideally, the reader will be inspired to ask new questions about the Qur'an and seek to find more connections that they were unaware of before and feel that they have a personal relationship with the Qur'an by being more familiar with it.

Each chapter of this book covers one Juz. While reading your Arabic Qur'an or your preferred translation, you should use *The Endless Banquet* as a guide to see the themes and connections for the āyāt that you are reading. One important point to keep in mind is that the Surahs of Qur'an are already divided into four major themes according to the Prophet ﷺ. He said, "I have been given the Seven Long Surahs in place of the Torah; I have been given the Hundreds in place of the *Zabūr;* and I have been given the Repeaters in place of the *Injīl;* and I have been given the unique privilege of the Partitioned Surahs." [Reported by al-Imam Aḥmad in his Musnad]

The Seven Long Surahs approximately cover the first ten Juz. These surahs contain a heavy emphasis on laws and the stories of the Prophets and their people, with particular detail given to the Jews and the Christians (i.e. People of the Book). The Surahs termed "The Hundreds" cover the next ten Juz. They emphasize the signs of Allah's existence in nature and an abundance of rational proofs for Allah's attributes. The last ten Juz cover the Repeaters and the Partitioned. The Repeaters highlight the proofs of the Day of Resurrection and magnitude of Allah's Power and control over creation, while the Partitioned are the shorter Surahs revealed in Makkah partitioned by "*Bismillāh Al-Raḥmān Al-Raḥīm*". They specifically address the Prophet Muhammad ﷺ while he was living through the hardships of spreading the Message in Makkah under severe persecution of the Quraish.

It is my hope that this work inspires a new generation of Qur'an readers, and that it rekindles a love for Qur'an inspired by its meanings, relevance, and connections that address the human condition. I pray that the Qur'an opens the hearts of all who read it, and that the *The Endless Banquet* becomes the key that helps unfasten the locks that have inhibited them from the impact of the reminder. May Allah make us all among those who are guided by its words and realize the promise of its rewards.

> Surely this Qur'an guides to that which is most upright and gives good news to the believers who do good that they shall have a great reward. [17:9]

Juz 1

THE HUMAN CONDITION

SURAH AL-FĀTIḤAH

It could be argued that *al-Fātiḥah* constitutes a summary of the Qur'an. Every part of the Qur'an can be linked back to an *āyah* from this surah. Examining the Qur'an from a higher level, it can be summarized as a book that teaches us two things: the relationship of Allah with His creation and our relationship with Him.

The beginning of *al-Fātiḥah* establishes the relationship between Allah and His creation: The first three *āyāt* revolve around four attributes of Allah. The first states that Allah is the Lord, and the second is that He is the Most Gracious (الرحمن), then the Most Merciful (الرحيم), and lastly the Master/King (مالك). The first attribute is associated with the relationship Allah has with nature. Not only does He nurture it, but He is also its caretaker. The meaning of His lordship flows directly into the meaning of being merciful (al-Raḥmān). Allah is merciful to all beings, regardless of their level of significance or insignificance. Following the second attribute is the description of Allah as the Most Merciful; the third attribute. This third attribute brings more nuance to His mercy by defining the specific mercy that is allotted to those who choose to worship and love Him. The fourth and final attribute, the Master/King, serves to define His relationship with His creation on the Day of Judgment. Altogether, these four attributes summarize the principles through which we understand the actions Allah takes at every stage of our existence.

The second half of the surah highlights our relationship with Allah and defines this through two categories. The first category defines the actions we should undertake both outwardly and inwardly. Outwardly, we are required to follow a lifestyle that allows us to worship Allah through rituals and by following the Shariah, and to do so purely for His sake (i.e. it is You we worship). Inwardly, we must rely on Him alone and not expect our actions to earn us salvation (i.e. from You we seek assistance).

The second category expands on the first by enhancing the definition of worshipping Allah and what our reliance should look like. Allah defines the nature of this path of worship and reliance based on the path of the righteous people who came before us. Simultaneously, we must avoid the path of people who have demonstrated extreme behaviour, such as that which incurs the anger of Allah or which leads to misguidance. All these extremes are elaborated on throughout the stories detailed in the Qur'an and will be discussed in future lessons *inshā'Allāh*.

SURAH AL-BAQARAH

ĀYĀT 1-20

The focus of the first Juz revolves around three categories of people based on their belief in Allah. One category consists of people who want to guard themselves from harm, thereby leading them to seek guidance, believe in the unseen, pray, give charity, and believe in all of the Prophets. Those belonging to the second category will be presented with guidance and disbelieve in it. Moreover, they will conceal it and refuse to allow its reason and light to penetrate their mind and heart. The last category is formed of the most complex group. In this category are people who outwardly affirm their belief – in keeping with the first group – however, inwardly they work to undermine the good work of the believers, thus siding with the second group of people who disbelieve. Allah describes them in great detail because they are the most conflicted group. They are also the worst group of the three because unlike those who are clearly disbelievers, they lie to Allah, to themselves, and to the believers, and it is they who do the most harm to humanity.

Allah then brings to light the proof of why humanity should believe in Him and His Messenger. Through this, He further emphasizes that the believers must follow the guidelines set by the Qur'an and the Sunnah of the Prophet and dictates how unreasonable and unnatural it would be to reject them.

And in case reason and logic are not enough to convince the reader, Allah then highlights the consequences of belief and disbelief. He describes the destiny of humanity in either Heaven or Hell based on where they stand regarding His revelation. He also provides a range of relevant examples, ranging from descriptions of a gnat and the human life cycle to all of creation itself, leaving no doubt of His authority.

Allah then transitions the reader to focus on the very beginning of humanity's existence and the responsibility placed upon humans to be good stewards. In this section, He introduces mankind's primary adversary, Iblīs, as well as our primary weakness: the human ego. Throughout the story, we observe how knowledge raises our rank whereas ignorance and following our lowly desires diminishes it. We also learn how we can recover from our mistakes and regain our rightful place with Allah. Overall, this story sets the stage for how all of humanity will struggle to follow guidance in the world to come.

At this point, Allah progresses to the subject of the Children of Israel. Here, just as He demonstrated His covenant with Ādam, He shows how He made a covenant with the Children of Israel, reminding them of how He saved them from the oppression of the Pharaoh under the guidance of Prophet Mūsā. Yet, as the reader will realize throughout the coming pages, salvation from worldly oppression is not sufficient without salvation from spiritual oppression of one's self.

ĀYĀT 51-66

Through the example of the Children of Israel, Allah demonstrates how spiritual oppression unfolds among believing communities, starting with ingratitude. Three primary areas of ingratitude are highlighted:

- Ingratitude for the blessing of worshipping Allah, by worshipping the calf and wanting to see Allah.

- Ingratitude for food, land, and drink, that resulted in the anger of Allah and worldly humiliation.

- Ingratitude for the sanctity of monumental sacred rituals such as the Sabbath.

ĀYĀT 67-80

Allah follows these *āyāt* by delving deeper into the psychology of those who are ungrateful. He describes how excessive questioning was employed by the Children of Israel with the intention of finding ways out of the religious responsibility of slaughtering the cow.

He then demonstrates how hearts can grow insensitive to the fear and awe of Allah.

Lastly, He shows how some of them intentionally distort the meaning of revelation and withhold information to transform the religion, making it fit one's lowly desires. Another group remains ignorant of what is detailed in the scriptures, thereby, purely relying on imagination and assumption to determine what Allah wants.

ĀYĀT 81-93

Allah elaborates on the nature of His covenants and how they can be broken. He portrays all the examples of how this happens in the following ways:

- By only using parts of the sacred law that give oppressors an advantage over the oppressed while ignoring other parts that require one to give up worldly possessions.

- Killing and lying about the Messengers who do not support one's lowly desires.

- Anticipating the assistance from Allah, but then rejecting it when it arrives because it does not fit their sense of worldly dominance.

- Only accepting older revelations while rejecting the current revelation of the Qur'an.

- Learning the truth and then blatantly disobeying it while continuing to claim faith, despite the warnings from Allah.

ĀYĀT 94-101

Through these *āyāt* Allah then reviews various characteristics of people who are predisposed to breaking the covenant. Of such individuals, there are those who love the life of this world more than the next, while others despise specific Messengers and angels of Allah. And then there are those who abandon the sacred laws of Allah and avoid following them as if they were never made aware of them.

ĀYĀT 95-123

Allah exposes the jealousy in the hearts of some people of other faiths. He then lays out examples of how they use differences in words and revelation to sow the seeds of discord within families and communities. All of these schemes are executed by drawing

> In the story of Ibrāhīm, Allah lays out the correct blueprint for Prophetic stewardship…

associations between their plots and the language of Divine guidance, thus, allowing them to develop misleading terminologies that lead to disbelief.

The first consequence of these plots is creating uncertainty in faith, through changing the sensibilities and the thinking process of believers who lack knowledge of revelation. However, the ultimate goal is for believers to abandon Islam altogether and renounce the guidance of Allah and His Messenger ﷺ. Allah then returns the focus back to the Children of Israel, reminding them of the blessings He has bestowed upon them as proof of why they, too, should follow this guidance.

The Children of Israel used to demonstrate how religion can be applied using incorrect means. Here, Allah exemplifies what fulfilling the purpose of religious stewardship truly looks like by introducing the story of Ibrāhīm and how he built the Kaaba. In the story of Ibrāhīm, Allah lays out the correct blueprint for Prophetic stewardship, including:

- Building a *masjid* as a place for people to unite in the worship of Allah.
- Facilitating security and sustenance for the community.
- Implementing intergenerational participation within worship and building a sense of community.
- Establishing religious education and spiritual purification.

The aforementioned legacy continues on through both lines of the Abrahamic lineage, ultimately becoming the foundation for the true religion of Allah that Muslims attribute to all the Prophets down to Prophet Muhammad peace and blessings be upon them all.

PERSONAL REFLECTIONS

Juz 2

THE NEW COVENANT

ĀYĀT 142-162

Continuing on from the theme of the Kaaba and its significance in religious history, through this Juz, Allah transitions the subject from ancient history directly to the lifetime of the Prophet Muhammad ﷺ. Furthermore, now that the paths of *al-Fātiḥah* have been demonstrated in the first Juz, Allah begins to introduce the covenant and laws that have been specified to the community of Prophet Muhammad ﷺ. These *āyāt* also define the various paths chosen by people in his time, based on their responses.

Through these specific *āyāt*, Allah initiates this section by detailing the issue of the changing of the *qiblah* from al-Quds in Jerusalem to the Kaaba in Makkah. Here, we are introduced to the hypocrites whom Allah described using the exact sentences they would say in response to the changing of the *qiblah*. Moreover, at this point, Allah reminds us that the Prophet does not have to answer to us regarding the laws of Allah. Rather, his role is to hold us accountable regarding whether we have followed Divine guidance or not. Through this lesson, we learn that the specific direction of the *qiblah* is not as important as He who dictates what the *qiblah* should be; namely, Allah. Unfortunately, for the hypocrites and the People of the Book, this was not enough to convince them that the Kaaba was a legitimate *qiblah*.

A common theme in these *āyāt* is that our accountability is not through the faith of communities that preceded us; rather, we are accountable to Allah in accordance with the message delivered by His Messenger. Therefore, even if the preceding faith communities reject him and his guidance, we must continue to be patient and hold fast onto the knowledge we have been given. Even if we are killed and afflicted with several tribulations, our patience and prayer will ultimately lead us to success. It is crucial to note that the *qiblah* is an essential part of staying focused on our spiritual direction, regardless of what is going on in the world.

Following on from the *qiblah*, Allah also sets the record straight regarding al-Ṣafā and al-Marwah and how they form part of the hajj and *'umrah* rites. Simultaneously, Allah chastises those who hide guidance from the people and persist in disbelief, a precedent that was set from the days of ignorance.

ĀYĀT 163-176

The majority of the lessons in these *āyāt* revolve around the theme of blindly following religion, allowing people to withhold and distort knowledge, and how these matters lead to Hell. Allah first declares that He is the only Creator, and that no other has authority over Him. Accordingly, He also declares that those who worship Him alone should struggle to avoid being led astray or guided by people who worship deities other than Him.

One example of the ways that such a struggle manifests itself is in dietary restrictions regarding meats. Allah states that the foods we eat must only be according to what He has made lawful. Moreover, we should not allow ourselves to follow the footsteps of one who is far from the guidance of Allah, both in actions and interpretations of the Divine law.

ĀYĀT 177-203

After setting the foundation of prayer and establishing Divine authority in lawgiving, Allah then directs the reader to consider how righteousness is a much broader matter than simply following the rules of prayer alone. Righteousness includes following guidance in determining:

- Who is most deserving of charity.
- How justice is delivered.
- How inheritance is divided.
- How to fast in Ramadan.
- Sighting the crescent moon to establish times for worship and avoiding tampering with time.
- Refraining from devising schemes to acquire each other's wealth unlawfully.
- How to conduct war.
- How to perform hajj.

ĀYĀT 204-222

Āyāt 204 to 222 centre around the theme of righteousness in interpersonal relationships, and how they are affected in various ways. Allah first establishes the tone by describing the characteristics of one who ultimately seeks to serve his own ego and contrasts this with one who serves the pleasure of Allah. Allah continues by instructing us to strive together towards attaining peace. He reminds us of the fate of the Children of Israel, and how humanity was once united but began using knowledge to dominate each other instead of improving themselves. Allah then answers five questions that people asked the Prophet:

- What should be given in charity and to whom.
- Permissibility of fighting during the sacred months while under religious persecution.
- Permissibility of gambling and alcohol.
- How to care for the orphan.
- The laws of menstruation.

ĀYĀT 223-242

Though this section spans several pages, it is simply an extension of the menstruation topic. Menstruation is a matter that directly affects both marriage and divorce and it is for this reason that Allah describes, in great detail, how women should be treated in marriage, the rules regarding how divorce can be conducted, and the regulations of the waiting period (*'iddah*). The text further covers teachings on how widows should conduct themselves and the waiting period following the death of a husband. It then sets guidelines on how men should respect women during this period, especially if they want to express interest in marrying them. Furthermore, Allah also mentions the rights of the mother regarding breastfeeding and child support.

ĀYĀT 243-252

Now that Allah has extensively discussed the laws governing rituals and interpersonal affairs, He transitions the topic to narrating stories to teach us how human beings interact with their Prophets and guidance when laws are given. He begins by relaying the story of the people who fled from the decree of Allah and died anyway. Through this story Allah demonstrates how He is in full control of all matters and that resisting the decree of Allah is futile and only leads to disappointment. From there, He relays the story of the Children of Israel and how they sought help from Allah. However, when Allah sent them Ṭālūt as an aid, most of them criticized Ṭālūt out of arrogance and refused to follow the guidance that he had relayed to them. In the end, only those who followed the laws were prepared for their victory. So when Ṭālūt and the minority of believers met Jālūt in the battlefield, Allah awarded them with victory and also blessed them with Dāwūd as a new Messenger and king.

Overall, this story demonstrates the need to follow the laws that Allah has specified. Moreover, it also describes how victory is gained through humility and allegiance to the Messenger that was sent to us, just as was done by the people who followed the laws of Ṭālūt.

> ...victory is gained through humility and allegiance to the Messenger ﷺ that was sent to us, just as was done by the people who followed the laws of Ṭālūt.

PERSONAL REFLECTIONS

Juz 3

THE POWER OF ALLAH

ĀYĀT
253-260

The start of this Juz continues with the theme of the Messengers as it follows on from the story of Ṭālūt and Dāwūd . Allah reminds us that all the Messengers were created by the same Creator. Thus, they should all be equally accepted as Messengers and this is a requirement of submitting to Allah. Further, Allah details how they are given different ranks based on the favours that He has bestowed upon them. Accepting this fact is an additional requirement on all believers. Accordingly, all believers must accept the hierarchy that Allah has established among the Messengers and, by extension, their miracles. Nevertheless, it is these very distinctions that create discord among people who view their Messengers as extensions of their egos instead of the favour Allah bestowed upon us. Such thinking leads to disputes between the various religious groups who attempt to establish the supremacy of *their* religion, by arguing that their Messenger is the only legitimate one. It follows, therefore, that those who pursue a religion other than Islam transform the role of their Messengers. Their Messengers were sent to them as facilitators who would lead them to submit to the guidance of Allah. Instead, their behaviour has transformed them into an obstacle that hinders them from submitting to the guidance of Prophet Muhammad ﷺ. Ultimately, this would not be a point of contention if they simply submitted to the hierarchy principle as established by Allah, rather than following their lowly desires.

Hence, in this section, Allah reminds us that He – not any Messenger of His – is the One who possesses ultimate power and is the only One who brings guidance and life. Only His guidance can lead a person to the light, and if anything other than Him is followed it will inevitably lead to darkness and doom. It is for this reason that we are introduced through this section to *āyah al-Kursī*. This point is further emphasized through different accounts: the debate that took place between Prophet Ibrāhīm and the king regarding who possesses the power of life and death; the story of the man who was resurrected after 100 years; and the story of Ibrāhīm and the resurrection of birds in his hands. Collectively, all of these stories revolve around the theme of recognizing the ultimate power of Allah, and that rejection of Him and His guidance will only lead to great loss and regret in the Hereafter.

In this section, Allah shifts the discussion to wealth, reiterating a theme from the first Juz where Allah had demonstrated how people are prone to 'selling out' their religion for material gain. We find that the downfall of many people of faith is brought about, not due to a lack of belief in Allah's ability to bring life and death, but rather due to their short-sightedness and by failing to understand how Allah controls all wealth. This leads to them "selling out" their religion for personal gain.

Therefore, Allah emphasizes here that just as He is the only one who creates life and death, He is also the only one who determines the granting and restricting of wealth. The matter detailed here is such an important issue that Allah dedicates the next twenty-one *āyāt* to teaching us the reality of wealth, how it affects one's belief, and the secret of its growth and diminishment.

To start, Allah discusses the act of giving of charity. He describes it as the surest way of increasing one's wealth, owing to the blessings that are bestowed by Allah upon the wealth of one who gives charity. However, this blessing has a condition; specifically, that the blessing is contingent on the reason the charity is given. Thus, such a charity must be given with sincere intentions and should not be given for worldly gain such as enhancing one's reputation. The intention will, therefore, determine how much blessing one receives when giving charity.

Next, Allah focuses on the form of charity that brings the most blessing. He emphasizes the need to avoid giving items that we do not need for charity out of fear of being stricken by poverty. In reality, Allah demonstrates that this type of thinking originates from the devil whose objective is to convince people to go to extremes to secure their worldly affairs. Meanwhile, Allah promises that He will ensure both our spiritual and material wellbeing if we simply follow the guidance on charity that He has outlined for us.

Allah then transitions to detailing how charity should be given, while also highlighting the best ways to give charity which lead to an elevation of the spirit. He also teaches us who the most blessed recipients of charity are and how to recognize them.

ĀYĀT
275-283

Now that Allah has established the conditions that should be met for a person's wealth to be blessed and increased, He turns our attention to how wealth can be diminished. Here Allah demonstrates that, just as charity is the single most powerful method of increasing wealth and spirit, interest is the single greatest method of destroying one's wealth and spirit.

Over an entire page, Allah gives us insight into the spiritual effect that interest has on those who acquire it, the arguments they use to justify it, and the clear religious prohibition of dealing with interest. Thus, Allah does not leave us in any doubt of the status interest holds with Him. Moreover, Allah teaches us that the reality of charity and interest are the exact opposite of what they appear to be: Allah will actually increase one's wealth through charity, even though it physically appears to decrease it, while conversely, He will destroy the wealth of a person who acquires interest, even though it seems like the wealth increases exponentially. Here, it is important to remember the lessons Allah previously taught us about His power over life and death, and that He controls the value and growth of all things in ways that we could never fully fathom. It is through these types of issues that faith is tested, and our perception of reality is challenged. In the end, it is for this reason that Divine guidance is essential to understanding how to make the best decisions that will bring us success.

Allah then draws our attention to another way that wealth is usurped; specifically, through faulty financial agreements involving interest or loans that are poorly documented or do not involve a collateral, thereby exposing the loanee and loaner to financial abuse. The significance of this topic is so great that Allah dedicates the longest *āyah* of the Qur'an to exploring its intricacies. In this *āyah*, Allah details measures of precaution that should be taken, including who should write the contract, how it should be written, witnesses who must be present during the agreement of the contract, protections for the scribes and the witnesses, and the spiritual considerations that are necessary. Lastly, He specifies how the loaner can protect himself financially by giving him the option of establishing a collateral in the contract in case the loan cannot be repaid.

ĀYĀT 284-286

Here we find ourselves at the end of *al-Baqarah*. We now have an in-depth understanding of the lessons to be gained from past communities. These lessons have been relayed, laws have been delivered, and the details of correct belief have been explained. Thus, at the close of *al-Baqarah*, Allah concludes by reminding us of how He will hold us accountable, and what He will hold us accountable for. He teaches us the *du'ā'* that we should make when seeking the best way to ask Allah for ease and compassion while we fulfil our obligation to serve Him.

SURAH ĀL 'IMRĀN

While surah *al-Baqarah* frequently addresses the Children of Israel and their history as a reference point for religious struggles, surah *Āl 'Imrān* addresses the belief of Christians for most of the *āyāt* leading up to the end of the Juz. The themes of these *āyāt* revolve around a conversation between the Prophet Muhammad ﷺ and a delegation of sixty Arab Christians from a region called Najran. This delegation approached the Prophet to examine the validity of his claim to Prophethood.

ĀYĀT 1-9

Allah immediately establishes His perfect attributes and the revelations that He has sent down to humanity, emphasizing that one must accept them all if they are to truly believe and save themselves from punishment. He also clarifies that He controls how people are created, foreshadowing the miraculous creations of Ādam, Yaḥyā, and 'Īsā, all of whom will be mentioned later.

Once His attributes and Books are affirmed, Allah then turns our attention to how those books are interpreted. He warns against certain groups trying to focus on ambiguous verses and building their theology based on that. Such interpretations oppose the reality Allah has established: that the true foundation of interpreting the Word of Allah must be through the clear and unambiguous verses. Adherence to the ambiguous verses stems from an imbalance in a person's heart that can only be cured by turning to Allah.

> ...material power will always be defeated when it opposes the power of faith and assistance from Allah. The allurement of worldly pleasures does not even compare to the pleasures of the Hereafter.

ĀYĀT 10-22

Before addressing the misconceptions of the People of the Book, Allah first demonstrates how success can only be attained through believing in Him. Moreover, He shows us that any benefits gained from disbelief will never serve as a protection from the punishment of Allah. He cites the fate of the Pharaoh and the battle of Badr as examples of how material power will always be defeated when it opposes the power of faith and assistance from Allah. The allurement of worldly pleasures does not even compare to the pleasures of the Hereafter. Thus, those who disbelieve in the guidance of Allah will be those who suffer great loss both in this world and in the next.

Once Allah has explained the reality of disbelievers, He then expounds upon the reality of believers, their characteristics, and their beliefs and true religion.

ĀYĀT 23-32

Allah then directs our attention to the People of the Book and how they avoid being held accountable by their own Book, highlighting the lack of faith they have in their own scripture. This section implies that the People of the Book avoid embracing its full guidance because they believe it would prevent them from maintaining their power. Such acts will not amount to any good in the Hereafter since Allah will serve justice in the Hereafter for those who reject guidance in this world.

Allah has full control over who attains power and who loses it just as clearly as He controls the day and the night, and the living and the dead. No amount of deception will be hidden from Allah. So regardless of claims of loving Allah, any attempt to follow disbelievers will surely be met with a tragic end. On the other hand, those who follow the Prophet Muhammad ﷺ will attain the true love of Allah because he represents the guidance of Allah. Thus, obeying him is tantamount to obeying Allah.

ĀYĀT 33-63

Now that the foundation has been set regarding the reality of belief and disbelief, Allah lays out the true stories of Prophetic lineages, specifically the family of 'Imrān . It is the family of 'Imrān that sits at the centre of the theological misunderstandings of the Judeo-Christian communities.

Through these *āyāt*, Allah clarifies the story of how Maryam was conceived and her relationship with Prophet Zakariyyā. Moreover, these *āyāt* also provide certain details of her miracles and the similarity between the birth of Yaḥyā, 'Īsā, and Ādam. Allah relates, in unambiguous terms, the details regarding the miracles of 'Īsā as a human Messenger like those before him. He also highlights his personal belief in Allah, and how Allah raised him and will liberate him from those who have used him to justify their disbelief in Allah. At this point, Allah details the evidence of the story of Prophet 'Īsā so clearly, that He orders Prophet Muhammad ﷺ to challenge the people of Najran to call upon Allah with him along with all of their families, and ask Allah to curse the one who is lying. This is the most emphatic expression of truth that people who claim faith in Allah can make. This expression also exposes the lack of confidence the people of Najran had in their own beliefs about 'Īsā.

ĀYĀT 64-83

Now that matters of theology have been addressed, Allah encourages the Muslims to identify the best approach for giving *da'wah* to the People of the Book. He directs them towards finding a common ground in their belief in Allah, and to focus on examining the religious legacy of Prophet Ibrāhīm. Here, Allah begins addressing the Christians directly, enjoining them to follow sound knowledge, and questioning their lack of will to accept His signs. He also exposes their hypocrisy and plots to mislead and deceive those who believe in Him.

ĀYĀT 84-91

Lastly, Allah commands us to adhere to the religion of submission to Allah (Islam) as was the religion of all the Prophets that have been sent by Him in the past. He also commands us to avoid following any path that takes us away from the guidance of Allah. Allah uses unambiguous terms to explicitly express the terrible outcomes of those who persist in oppressing themselves in darkness. However, salvation is open to those who decide to return to Him and rectify their ways. Ultimately, the greatest regrets will be held by those who meet Allah in a state of disbelief. It is those individuals who will have nothing to protect themselves from the punishment once their time has run out. It is only in this world that one can sacrifice all things beloved to them to attain righteousness.

PERSONAL REFLECTIONS

Juz 4

PROTECTING THE COMMUNITY

ĀYĀT 92-99

Now that Allah has comprehensively explained the major matters of history and theology, He begins to direct the People of the Book to learn from the experience of the Children of Israel who unnecessarily constricted their own laws and consequently distorted the religion of Allah.

In contrast to the Children of Israel, Allah describes the way of Prophet Ibrāhīm as a symbol of true religion. Additionally, He highlights the universal nature of his Prophethood, the Kaaba, and the station of Ibrāhīm, all of which the Children of Israel and Christians should acknowledge. Hence, Allah rhetorically asks why they reject these signs and prevent people from following the correct path to Allah.

ĀYĀT 100-120

Following on from the previous section, Allah warns the believers against obeying certain factions of the People of the Book, reminding us that we already have a Messenger with Divine guidance in the form of the Qur'an. Moreover, He also reminds us to hold fast to practicing our religion until the day we die.

It is worth noting here that this guidance is not complete if it is only followed individualistically. Hence, Allah advises us believers to hold fast to the Qur'an as a community, not as separate groups. He also asks us to be united under the same guidance. Such solidarity will give us the strength we need to remain resilient under the pressure of those who disbelieve. Furthermore, we should be united in our effort to improve humanity as a whole; enjoining the right and forbidding the wrong. We should also recall that illumination and mercy in the Hereafter is contingent on holding fast to our religious dedication.

It is this exact same mission that Allah enjoins for the Children of Israel and for the Christians, yet most do not adhere to it. Instead, they disbelieved and attempted to kill their Messengers – including Prophet Muhammad ﷺ. A minority of them, however, accepted the guidance of Prophet Muhammad ﷺ and followed the religious guidelines set by the revelation of the Qur'an.

With all these realities mentioned, Allah commands us to avoid entrusting ourselves to those who have shown animosity towards us. Furthermore, Allah reminds us that true protection only comes from Him, and that our *taqwā* will ultimately save us from the plots of our enemies. As proof of this, Allah cites the Battle of Badr as an example of how He brings victory to the believers by sending angels to support and protect them. Finally, once again Allah emphasizes to us that He controls the outcome of everything, so there is no need to turn to anyone but Him for guidance.

ĀYĀT 121-148

Even if the believers resist the temptation of entrusting themselves to the People of the Book, they may still suffer the same consequence and fall into the same pitfalls of the faith communities that preceded them. Accordingly, these *āyāt* offer a temporary shift of focus towards discussing the practices that would lead to the downfall of the believers, a matter that must be avoided.

The first matter involves avoiding the practice of dealing in interest; a topic that was discussed extensively at the end of Surah *al-Baqarah*. Re-iterating this topic here serves to emphasize the gravity of the matter. Moreover, just as charity was mentioned as the countermeasure to interest, here it is mentioned again in combination with forgiving and seeking forgiveness as a means of attaining Paradise. Allah tells us to observe how the nations preceding us were tested, indicating that we should use them as reference points from which we can learn the consequence of such practices. These lessons would also educate us on who ultimately succeeded and died upon the truth as Allah will test us in the same way.

From there, foreshadowing the topic of Uhud, Allah introduces one of the greatest tests of faith: the coming of the Prophet's eventual death. Allah instructs us that we cannot act like those before us who went to extremes at the death of their Prophet by either making his nature greater than a Messenger or abandoning the religion altogether. Rather, Allah shows us the example of those who were steadfast and sought aid in the face of matters of death. These were the people of excellence.

Once again Allah reiterates how believers should not be led astray by following the disbelievers. Instead, they should rely on Allah as their Saviour. On this occasion, He cites the Battle of Uhud as an example. Several lessons are taught through this event:

- Allah takes charge of striking fear into the hearts of the disbelievers, the enemy, regardless of the odds that are in their favour. Thereby, Allah ensures the success of the community of faith in the face of opposition. It is therefore futile for believers to seek success by following the way of disbelievers in religion.

- Seeking material gain by leaving the guidance of the Prophet will only lead to failure. Allah demonstrates how this came to be at Uhud, when their fortune immediately changed for the worst when they left the Prophet for worldly possessions.

- The decree of Allah is inevitable, so abandoning one's responsibilities to avoid death will only lead to the same result. The only difference is whether one meets death in a state of obedience or a state of disobedience.

- Death is not the ultimate failure. Disbelief is. In fact, the greatest success lies in dying in a state of obedience, thereby, leading one to gain the forgiveness and mercy of Allah. Therefore, taking sinful measures to avoid death brings no benefit.

- Believers have the greatest blessing bestowed upon them through their connection to Prophet Muhammad ﷺ to whom Divine assistance is promised. Therefore, any tribulation that believers experience is due to an internal deficiency caused by our own shortcomings, or by the infiltration of hypocrisy. All of these examples are revealed to us through our reactions to experiencing hardships.

In the end, those of us who sacrifice and die for Allah will have the ultimate reward. Moreover, despite how daunting things might seem in this world, our faith in the Hereafter will allow us to overcome our hardships and look forward to being rewarded by Allah for our sacrifice.

Allah knows that people often turn away from guidance and follow those who disbelieve to avoid death and defeat. It is for this reason that Allah addresses the reality of what is perceived as "defeat" in this world with these āyāt. In reality, what disbelievers consider to be defeat in death is actually success for the believer. This is because the martyr is a person who has fulfilled their responsibility to Allah and has made the ultimate sacrifice in his obedience to the Messenger, thereby gaining the superior reward. Those who understand this reality look forward to experiencing it, while those who lack faith succumb to their internal fear and the whispers of shayṭān.

Allah also addresses what is perceived by disbelievers as "success" in the form of extensive comfort and enjoyment in this world. In reality, Allah is just giving them more time to dig deeper into sin, which will only compound their regret and punishment in the end. Conversely, the trials experienced by believers are not a punishment. Rather, they are a weeding out process separating the sincere from the hypocrites. Based on this understanding, the wealthy miser is not actually benefitting himself by holding back, but rather only binding himself more to his inevitable punishment.

ĀYĀT 181-200

In this section, Allah lays out why it is unreasonable for believers to set out to appease the People of the Book. Allah cites the audacity of those who attribute poverty to Allah, and their demands to see specific miracles, even though they rejected and killed the previous Prophets who came with the miracles they requested. Therefore, we should not be surprised by their disapproval and verbal abuse. These are the same people who betrayed their own religion and sold out their guidance for worldly gain. The likes of these people will undoubtedly be the losers when their death inevitably arrives.

On the other hand, the true believers are those who see the clear signs of their Lord all around them. As a consequence, they are in constant remembrance of Him in every situation. Instead of turning to disbelievers for success, they pray to Allah to safeguard them from punishment whilst following the guidance of the Messenger. It is due to this sincere devotion that Allah answers their call and rewards them for all of their struggles with something far greater than the temporary comforts that He entertains the disbelievers with in this world. In the end, the only people among the Children of Israel and Christians that will gain this reward are those who follow the same guidance from Prophet Muhammad ﷺ. Guidance that is in keeping with that sent in their own scriptures, as that is the only path of success.

SURAH AL-NISĀ'

ĀYĀT
1-14

While Surah Āl 'Imrān heavily focused on the social and political dynamics between the Muslims and the People of the Book, Surah al-Nisā' shifts the focus to the personal dynamics between families. It begins by reminding us that Allah created us in a way in which we are all essentially related. Thus, familial relationships are part of our human identity and must be respected as a sacred bond. Each member of the family has sacred rights that must be maintained. Therefore, Allah introduces the rights of women and children. Men were generally created to have a natural physical dominance over them, and therefore, have the greatest responsibility to protect their rights.

Firstly, Allah makes mention of the rights of children, specifically those whom Allah has taken that family bond away from, namely the orphan. We must take special care in watching over them and their affairs, particularly in how their wealth is managed. Since the capital of an orphan's wealth is almost exclusively acquired through inheritance, the issue of inheritance needs to be addressed first so that it is not left up to others to interpret it to their own advantage. Allah delves into the minute details regarding the rightful shares due to each of the immediate family members of the deceased, highlighting that these guidelines are clear boundaries that must not be violated.

Next, Allah instructs the community on how to safeguard the reputation of their women by protecting them from slander and false accusations of sexual misconduct. Simultaneously, He describes the nature of repentance for those who commit sexual deviance and shows that the door of forgiveness is always open as long as the individual is not at the cusp of death. Allah follows this by dismantling the oppressive practices of the Arabs who used to inherit women without consent, treat them poorly in marriages, or usurp their wealth. He also abolishes incestuous marriages by specifying every type of relationship that falls under that category.

> ...true believers are those who see the clear signs of their Lord all around them. As a consequence, they are in constant remembrance of Him in every situation.

PERSONAL REFLECTIONS

Juz 5

SOCIAL REFORM

ĀYĀT 24-32

Continuing on from the end of Juz 4 and the instructions Allah has set on safeguarding the sanctity of women, Allah establishes the right of women to have dowries, and to marry in a dignified public manner that maintains their good reputation. In the event that a person violates the sanctity that Allah gave them, Allah reminds us of the forms of repentance that can restore their status with Allah and that the door of repentance is always open and made easy for us.

Since the protection of dowries falls within the broader category of financial rights, Allah emphasizes that it is prohibited to usurp the wealth of anyone. He further discourages us from envying the different favours that He has given men and women, and that each have their share of what is good in their own way. The more we understand this concept, the more people would be safeguarded from scheming and violating each other's rights for the sake of "getting ahead" in this life. Moreover, the rulings of this sections also apply to family relationships, where inheritance is often unlawfully seized or where family members use their blood relationships to wrongfully take advantage of each other.

ĀYĀT 33-57

In this section, Allah turns our attention to safeguarding the sanctity of His Word because when that is violated, the rights of humanity cannot be appropriately upheld.

The section begins with instructions on preserving the sanctity of our minds by avoiding alcohol – especially during prayer – and also preserving the sanctity of prayer spaces (the *masjids*). As long as the mind is clear and the places of worship are pure, the Book of Allah will remain protected from being tampered with.

In case we needed a good reminder of why this was vital, Allah continues by reminding us that we should take heed from the example of the majority of the People of the Book. They sold out their religion and distorted their scripture by twisting words to undermine the faith. Such people will be cursed if they do not repent, for Allah makes it clear that polytheism is the only sin which will not be forgiven if one were to die upon it. The origin of such unforgiveable acts stems from the lies they told about Allah Himself even though they were once upon guidance. Despite this, they continue to claim righteousness while harbouring hatred and jealousy towards those who follow the truth, further compounding their lies. For this reason, they are allotted a specific punishment if they do not repent. The believers, on the other hand, will have the greatest reward.

ĀYĀT 58-70

Allah makes it clear that we must not stop at simply preserving the integrity of the Qur'an. Rather, leaders must strive to govern according to its guidelines and deliver rights where they are due.

Once again, He uses the People of the Book as an example of what it looks like when the governance of Allah is abandoned for the governance of false authorities, and how hypocrites will jump at the opportunity to support the latter at the believers' expense. Hence, Allah reminds us that our belief is contingent upon governing our affairs according to the judgement of Prophet Muhammad . Ultimately, we would discover that such actions would be in our best interest, even if it means we must put our own lives on the line or leave the comfort of our homes.

ĀYĀT 71-86

To ensure the protection and upholding of the rights of the vulnerable, and the preservation of the Qur'an and our religious way of governance, men must be willing to defend these matters with their lives. Consequently, warfare was legislated and regulated as a means of protecting the wellbeing of the believing community. These are the matters that form the focus of this section.

Fighting for the sake of protecting the religion of Allah, the right to worship Him alone, and to propagate Divine guidance will always prevail over fighting for falsehood. Hence, Allah addresses the problem with people who fear defeat and death at the hands of those who fight for falsehood. Their cowardice is counterproductive because death is inevitable, and any harm that they suffer will only be due to their disobedience. If we seek success, then the only way to succeed is to serve Allah, because He is the only source of good.

Another important point is that obedience to the Messenger of Allah is equivalent to obedience to Allah. Therefore, Divine success also resides in following and fighting for the Messenger – or those who are rightfully leading in his place. Since this is a critical part of a believer's salvation, Allah reminds the Prophet to encourage the believers to fight with him to secure their own success with Allah against their enemies.

Now that warfare has been legislated, Allah regulates who can be fought against.

Starting with turncoats and clear enemies, He begins by highlighting the difference between those who openly fight and work against the believers versus those who seek to make peace and establish treaties. The former can be fought against while with the latter it is necessary for peace to be maintained.

As for those who believe, they must not be fought against. If they are killed by accident, then Allah details in this section the forms of compensation that must be made to set things right, depending on the situation of the victim and the perpetrator. As for the intentional murder of a believer, the consequences of this act will be the most severe with Allah because these people are the closest to Him.

> Allah will always turn the hypocrite's schemes back against them, so they only really undermine themselves.

ĀYĀT 95-104

In this section, our attention is shifted from the status of those who are fought, to the status of those who fight and migrate for the sake of Allah.

Firstly, Allah distinguishes the ranks of those who fight for His sake over those who stay behind, and then further distinguishes between those who stay behind for legitimate reasons and those who lack any legitimate reason.

Furthermore, as an assurance for individuals who are too suppressed to fight and migrate for religious freedom, thus missing out on the reward of fighting for His cause, Allah gives good tidings that their migration will also be rewarded greatly. Allah bestows His mercy upon them by allowing them to shorten their prayers to ease their travelling, just as He legislates a modified prayer for those who fight in the battlefield.

ĀYĀT 105-126

Now that Allah has established the rights of the people and the ways those rights should be protected, He transitions the subject from those who must be fought against to the hypocrites present among the ranks. The hypocrites are people whom the believers cannot fight. Although they continue to scheme from within, they are not clear enemies and so they must be tolerated.

The reality is that their schemes never actually undermine the Prophet because Allah provides Divine protection for him and those who follow him. On the other hand, Allah will always turn the hypocrite's schemes back against them, so they only really undermine themselves.

With that being said, Allah shows that there is still hope for the hypocrites. If they seek forgiveness, they can still be forgiven. However, those who deflect the blame away from themselves will be held fully accountable for their sins.

Allah also elaborates how most plots have no benefit in them, other than those which clearly improve society, and that opposing the Prophet and the way of the believers will only lead to one being punished. He then details how those who plot evil are themselves the victims of the greater plot of *shayṭān* while those who are righteous and follow the Prophet are destined to bliss.

ĀYĀT 127-130

Previously, Allah gave men broad instructions on how to protect their society both externally and internally. Now He brings the subject back to the protection of the women and orphans. In this section, He details the measures that women can take to protect themselves from neglectful and abusive husbands. It is worth noting that this topic is relevant at this juncture, because up until this point the reader might assume that Allah has placed all authority of marital affairs in the hands of men alone. Rather, Allah has given women their share of self-determination, to protect themselves and take matters into their own hands when they encounter men who have neglected and failed to fulfil the responsibilities Allah gave them. Furthermore, Allah promises that He will enrich those men and women who felt divorce was necessary to avoid further harm. This further liberates women from the pressure of feeling obligated to remain in relationships where their rights are not being upheld.

ĀYĀT 131-147

Historically, as communities of faith gain greater authority and become more powerful, they are more likely to become the victim of their own vices than to be defeated by external enemies. Accordingly, Allah emphasizes the importance of adhering to Divine guidance for our own sake, and not obsessing over material gain at the expense of our Hereafter, lest we be replaced by other people. Such behaviour requires a level of self-accountability that will test our commitment to truth. Therefore, it is vital for us to be capable of recognizing hypocrisy, thereby ensuring we do not fall into it in our attempts to avoid the truth. Allah dedicates a portion of the concluding *āyāt* to specifically describe the hypocrites. Among the signs of hypocrisy are:

- Making mockery of the religion.
- Habitual alternating between belief and disbelief.
- Seeking honour in the authority of disbelievers over believers.
- Being opportunistic and switching sides between believers and disbelievers when it is convenient.
- Being religiously ambiguous.

In the end, the hypocrites will be in the lowest depths of Hell. Yet, even for them, there is still time to repent and to be forgiven before their death. Such forgiveness is possible despite all the harm and sins committed because Allah wants them to return to Him so that He may show them His mercy. Ultimately, His mercy outweighs His wrath.

PERSONAL REFLECTIONS

Juz 6

UPHOLDING THE RELIGION

ĀYĀT 148-161

The previous *āyāt,* at the end of Juz 5, highlight the fact that the believers will have to tolerate the internal animosity of the hypocrites. On the other hand, the subsequent *āyāt* in this segment will teach us about the infractions of the People of the Book, starting with the Children of Israel who only acknowledge the Prophets they prefer. Through this, Allah will teach us how to respond to those who harm us, whether internally or externally.

In the beginning of this section, we are instructed to be careful with how we speak and to avoid using harmful words against innocent people. In fact, it is not only important to speak good, but also to be forgiving as opposed to retaliating out of revenge.

This is the type of patience that the Prophet demonstrated when the Children of Israel requested for him to bring a traditional book like that of Mūsā, as if that would be a sufficient sign to convince them to become believers. Allah reminds us that, historically, they were given even greater signs but the Children of Israel persisted in their disbelief, killed Prophets, and lied about the death of Prophet 'Īsā before Prophet Muhammad ﷺ. In addition, they already had laws that had been given to them before, but they violated them by taking interest and usurping people's wealth, so what difference would another book really make?

ĀYĀT 162-176

Allah then affirms that there are people who do not need new signs to prove the authenticity of the Prophet and the truth of his speech. The Qur'an is sufficient evidence for them. Moreover, the entire unseen realm also affirms this fact. Allah draws links between all the previous Prophets and Prophet Muhammad ﷺ by demonstrating that there is no difference between their messages. Therefore, disbelieving in Prophet Muhammad ﷺ would be akin to disbelieving in all of them and will only lead to Hell.

As for the Christians, they – like the Children of Israel – have also made incorrect statements about Prophet 'Īsā: calling him the begotten son of Allah and believing in the Trinity. Allah makes it clear that only those who have correct belief in 'Īsā, in agreement with the truth whilst also performing righteous deeds, will be rewarded. In contrast, those who become arrogant and refuse to accept the truth will be punished.

In summary, after relating the history of how the previous communities rejected their Messengers, Allah shows that the Prophet has sufficient evidence that he is indeed the Messenger of Allah. All that is required from humanity is to believe in him and worship Allah alone.

With that, Allah ends the surah with more laws, reminding us that he has provided us with all the answers we need to remain on the straight path (ṣirāṭ al-mustaqīm). All we have to do is believe and follow it.

SURAH AL-MĀ'IDAH

ĀYĀT
1-5

While Surah *al-Nisā'* begins by discussing laws that protect society and relationships between people, Surah *al-Mā'idah* opens with a discussion on our relationship with food, particularly the animals we consume. In this surah, Allah presents a detailed list of the types of meats that are forbidden, paralleling the list of relationships that are forbidden in Surah *al-Nisā'*. He also states the rules of hunting; explaining in what situations hunting is allowed during the hajj season, the kinds of hunting animals that can be used, and how the People of the Book can slaughter these animals for us and that is lawful. This final point is similar to other associations with the People of the Book Allah, such as having permission to marry their women.

ĀYĀT 6-16

In a similar way that He addressed the Children of Israel in Surah *al-Baqarah*, Allah now addresses the current believers. He details specific instructions on how to worship with extra details on purification. He also reminds us of the blessing He has bestowed in the form of a new covenant and promises a great reward for upholding it. Moreover, He highlights how He extends His blessing by protecting the believers from their enemies.

On the other hand, He warns us against treating our covenant in the same manner as the Children of Israel. He gave them similar instructions yet they broke their covenant, distorted it, and neglected its preservation. Thus most of them developed insensitive and treacherous hearts.

He also warns us of treating our covenant like the Christians did, who also neglected the preservation of their Book, thereby developing hatred for each other.

After outlining their shortcomings, He then reminds both groups that Prophet Muhammad has come to set the record straight and can guide them to rectify their ways if they follow him as Muslims.

ĀYĀT 17-26

Allah continues to show how the People of the Book have broken their covenants by specifying how both the Children of Israel and the Christians deviated, even though they both claim the exclusive love of Allah. The Christians distorted their theology altogether, by equating the Messiah to Allah, while the Children of Israel never fully accepted the teachings of Prophet Mūsā. The Children of Israel used every opportunity they could to disobey him when sacrifices were required. Just as Allah blessed us with sacred land and a Prophet, the People of the Book received similar blessings in the past. But when they were required to make the necessary sacrifices to follow the guidance and accept their blessings, they refused to take action, so Allah withheld it from them for forty years.

The lesson we learn from this story is that we have the responsibility of preventing people from distorting our theology and laws. We must also make the necessary sacrifices to accept our blessings and follow the guidance of Prophet Muhammad ﷺ. Otherwise, we will experience the same loss as the communities that came before us.

ĀYĀT 27-40

For the majority of the succeeding sections, Allah provides us with examples and details on how faith communities failed to uphold their religion.

In this section He relates the story of Qābīl and Hābīl, and how Qābīl's crime of murder became a sin which set the precedent for every murder that came after it.

Hence, any unrepentant rebels from the community who take up arms to kill the Prophet and the innocent must be made into an example to deter others from following suit and to halt the cycles of murder. Similarly, those who steal should be made into an example to deter others from stealing and so that momentum does not build up for future crimes.

ĀYĀT 41-57

Here, Allah highlights how guidance is abandoned, and how it is related to the connection between what we consume and what we produce. This is why the laws of food are so vital.

As an example, Allah tells the Prophet not to be surprised by hypocrites when they rush to disbelief. They have fallen into the same habits as the Children of Israel, who consumed unlawful matter and produce, through their mental and physical diet, by accepting lies and unlawful food. Therefore, it only follows that they, in turn, produce lies about religion and exhibit unlawful actions.

He then demonstrates how the Children of Israel further abandoned their religion by not following the laws of the Torah, despite the Torah being sent as a light and guidance for them. Allah also details how the Christians followed the same path by abandoning the Injīl similarly to how the Children of Israel abandoned the Torah.

Allah turns the focus to us and our Book and reminds us that we must live according to the guidance in the Qur'an and that we should not abandon its laws, like those before us, by seeking out laws of ignorance that suit our desires.

Since hypocrites are the ones who lead the charge to abandon religious law, this section highlights the reasons and signs of hypocrisy. In sum, complete hypocrisy is when a person publicly declares themselves as a Muslim, yet they privately place their spiritual allegiance with disbelievers, such as the Children of Israel and the Christians. In doing so they believe they can find protection in and benefit from both groups at the same time. Hence, Allah warns them of the punishment that they will receive and that their entire community will be replaced if they persist in their transgression.

ĀYĀT 58-71

Allah further points out to the hypocrites that it is futile to follow the lead of the People of the Book, who do not take their own religion or Allah seriously and mock the *adhān* when they hear it.

They already harbour hypocrisy in their own religion, making undeserved declarations of spiritual purity, eating unlawful foods, and enthusiastically racing to sinful and disbelieving deeds (such as saying that the hands of Allah are tied), spreading corruption, and inciting war.

Despite all of this, Allah still opens the doors of forgiveness for them, advising them that if they just believed in Prophet Muhammad ﷺ and upheld the original guidance of the Torah and Injīl as it was revealed, Allah would still shower them with blessings.

Hence, Allah commands us to proclaim the truth through the guidance that He has given us, and to hold the Children of Israel and the Christians accountable for the guidance that was given to them, which affirms the truth of the message of Prophet Muhammad ﷺ, until they believe.

ĀYĀT 72-81

In the last section, Allah said that people of previous religions would be rewarded if they believed. Because of this, some assume that they can take this statement and claim that they do not have to follow Prophet Muhammad ﷺ at all. Consequently, Allah states in unambiguous terms that those who equate ʿĪsā with Allah are disbelievers, and that those who believe in the Trinity are also disbelievers. He definitively states that ʿĪsā and Maryam were human beings, thereby leaving no doubt about the truth of the matter.

Since the Christians were originally taught by the Children of Israel, Allah discourages them from trusting the Jewish narrative by reminding them that the Children of Israel were cursed by some of their own Prophets, and that they did not uphold their own religion. Moreover, instead of following Prophet Muhammad ﷺ, they preferred the laws of the disbelievers over Divine guidance. Now, the only way for them to save themselves is to follow Prophet Muhammad ﷺ.

"We have the responsibility of preventing people from distorting our theology and laws. We must also make the necessary sacrifices to accept our blessings and follow the guidance of Prophet Muhammad ﷺ.

PERSONAL REFLECTIONS

Juz 7

THE TRANSCENDENCE OF ALLAH

ĀYĀT 82-91

Following on from the end of Juz 6, Allah continues on the subject about the Christians and how they have a greater natural affinity to the Qur'an and Prophet Muhammad ﷺ than the Children of Israel. Of the two groups, they are the likeliest prospects when it comes to becoming followers of Prophet Muhammad ﷺ.

Allah then shifts our attention to Divine law, addressing the believers and giving them guidance that contradicts the practices of the People of the Book. Accordingly, Muslims should refrain from imposing unnecessary dietary restrictions on themselves, they should take their contractual oaths seriously, and they should avoid gambling and alcohol altogether because they are weapons of *shayṭān*.

ĀYĀT 92-108

Now that the surah is coming to an end, the discussion comes full circle, returning to the regulations on food, specifically regarding the animals hunted during hajj or in the Sacred Grounds. Surprisingly, this is one of the most unique aspects of the surah. Unlike most other legal systems, the rights of animals here are so unique that the intentional killing of an animal calls for significant reparations akin to those of killing a human being. The reason for this lies in the sanctity of the Sacred Grounds and months. It is also a test that gauges how committed we are to obeying Allah over our own desires to consume certain foods, and the strength of our belief in the judgement of Allah on which food is filthy and which is pure.

Through His infinite wisdom, Allah knows that our unnecessary questioning and superstitions can be a major reason for laws becoming more severe and restricted, similar to how it was with the Children of Israel. Therefore, Allah discourages us from engaging in these practices and also from worrying about the harm that the people of misguidance can cause, so long as we adhere to His guidance.

Demonstrating how thorough His guidance and legal protection is, Allah shows us how His laws not only protect our best interests in life, but also in death. Here, He elaborates on how, even when a person has died away from his homeland, a person's will should be protected from being tampered with, citing the process of how witnesses of a will should be vetted.

ĀYĀT 109-120

At a higher level, Allah shows how He also protects the legacy of the Messengers, relating the story of the miracles of Prophet ʿĪsā, and how he interacted with his disciples. Interestingly, He describes how the disciples asked ʿĪsā for a repast so they could verify it as a sign, and it would be a returning blessing for each generation. Yet, we find that the people who came after Prophet ʿĪsā abandoned the guidance he had given them and made up lies about him which Allah will interrogate them about on the Day of Judgment.

Similarly, Allah has presented us with the Qu'ran, with guidance that every generation can benefit from in unique ways. Allah has blessed us with clear guidance on every matter from food to wills, including the truth regarding the life of Prophet ʿĪsā. Therefore, we should take heed of this message and learn from the mistakes of the People of the Book. We should follow the guidance that Allah has given us in the way that He dictates, for our own salvation.

SURAH AL-ANʿĀM

In this surah, Allah begins by detailing various different signs of His power; leaving no doubt that He is the Creator of the heavens and the earth.

He speaks about the origin of our creation, how He showered blessings on sinful civilizations before us who were destroyed and have been replaced by others. Moreover, He demonstrates that no matter how great a miracle they experience, they will continue to not believe, even if they could touch revelation or if an angel were sent to them.

He encourages us to learn from the outcome of the societies that preceded us and to consider who controls and who initiated the universe. If we actually pondered on all of the signs around us, it would behove us to know that He is the only source of benefit and harm, and that He is a sufficient witness for truth.

ĀYĀT 20-35

Now that numerous signs of the lordship of Allah have been established, He shifts our focus to those who reject submitting to Him. Those who have received revelations before the Qur'an are those who are also more knowledgeable of the Prophet. It therefore follows that they have no valid reason to reject him, and their lies will be exposed to them on the Day of Judgement.

Allah continues by detailing the reality of their situation in this life and in the next. They cut themselves off from accepting any sign from the Prophet, while on the Day of Judgment they will be full of regret.

Hence, in this section, Allah explains how deceiving the life of this world is, and how disappointed the Prophet is in his inability to convince people of the truth and the coming consequences. Allah reassures him that their disbelief is not due to a lack of his teachings – because the signs of the truth are clear – rather, their disbelief is due to them lacking open hearts, and that is something he cannot change. Only people who are willing to listen to the truth will answer his call.

"Only people who are willing to listen to the truth will answer his call.

ĀYĀT 36-58

In this section, Allah responds to another demand from the disbelievers for a miracle – as if they seek to test how powerful Allah is.

Allah replies by listing miracles He has already manifested; the organization of the animal kingdom, the fact that He is who they turn to in times of dire need, all the stories of the societies who challenged the signs of Allah, and the senses of hearing and sight. Then He declares how severe the punishment will be for the people who reject Prophet Muhammad ﷺ.

In contrast, Allah describes those who are receptive to His signs, instructing the Prophet to remain close to them and treat them well, for they are usually those who are looked down upon by society.

Finally, Allah teaches the Prophet how to respond to his challengers; instructing him to make it clear that he does not make demands to Allah, nor will he succumb to the demands of the disbelievers' desires.

ĀYĀT 59-72

In these *āyāt*, Allah describes Himself in detail, thereby, providing us with an understanding of how powerful His attributes are. He speaks about His knowledge of the most minute details of creation, His power over our life, death, and resurrection, and how He can encompass us in punishment in any way He wills.

All of this proves how futile the efforts of the disbelievers are against the infinite power of Allah. It is for this reason that Allah tells the Prophet to leave the disbelievers to the games they play with this religion and that this would be to their detriment if they refuse to take guidance from him. Instead, he must simply relay the message to them and focus on worshipping Allah and doing righteous deeds. In the end, they will see the reality of who Allah is on the Day of Judgment.

ĀYĀT 73-90

In this section, Allah then continues by giving us an example of how this situation with the disbelievers plays out. In this example, Allah relays to us the story of Prophet Ibrāhīm in which he debates with his people about the reality of Allah. Here, He relates the famous story of Ibrāhīm pointing at the sun, moon, and stars, making logical arguments for why they cannot be worshipped as the Creator. These are obvious signs for people who use intellectual judgement. Yet, here we see his community still rejecting his message despite the clear logical proofs provided by Prophet Ibrāhīm. Instead of acceding to his message they threatened him with their idols' retaliation.

Allah then shows that this is part of the same legacy of all the Prophets, all of whom were related, and highlights the most well-known among them, proving that the Prophet's situation is not unusual, rather it is proof that he is indeed following the right path as those before him.

ĀYĀT 91-94

Regarding the disbelievers, the reality is that they hold a very low opinion of Allah and lack belief in the Hereafter. It is for this reason that they refuse to believe that He would send a Messenger to them. It is also why some of them have the audacity to falsely claim Prophethood, as if they will not be expected to have to answer to Allah in the end.

Allah will bring each person by themselves to answer for what they have done. After all their lies and deception in this world, no one will be able to come to aid the disbelievers, nor will they be in a position to help. Only those who submitted to Allah in this life will be in a position to gain His mercy in the next.

ĀYĀT 95-111

As this Juz comes to a close, Allah directs the reader to reflect on His attributes and to develop greater certainty in His power. He demonstrates His power through various means: from details as minute as how seeds are split, to the astronomical shifts of the universe, the power to bring forth innumerable numbers of people from a single soul, and the entire atmospheric process that controls the growth of vegetation.

How then, could a disbeliever claim that an idol, or man, or jinn can accomplish any of these miracles? Clearly, one who makes that argument is spiritually and intellectually blinded by ego and desire. So Allah reassures the Prophet not to take responsibility for their arrogance when they repeatedly demand to see signs because no matter what sign Allah gives them, they will not believe. Neither should we denigrate their idols only to make them even more arrogant. Instead, follow the guidance that has been given and let them have the freedom to find out the truth themselves in the next life.

PERSONAL REFLECTIONS

Juz 8

HISTORY REPEATS

ĀYĀT 112-132

The eighth Juz begins by exemplifying the consistent pattern of struggles faced by the Prophets, who call towards guidance, at the hands of the devils, who call to misguidance. This dichotomy of leadership was established by Allah as part of the human experience to give us the choice and freedom to worship Him out of love and not by force.

Hence, Allah supports the Prophet with instructions and strategies to help convince people to follow this religion which is, above all, in their best interest. However, Allah also reminds him that their disregard is not unexpected: most people in his lifetime will not believe in him. Moreover, many of them will prefer distracting you with ignorance and assumption.

Next, Allah revisits an example which is very relevant to the struggle between guidance and misguidance: the regulations regarding meats. Since animals are living beings like us and, therefore, have a level of sanctity, Allah has only given us permission to kill certain animals for food. Those who follow guidance should only consume the meat of those animals that have been slaughtered in a sacred manner; a condition for making them permissible to eat. Those who follow their desires and reject guidance eat animals killed aimlessly, without following the sacred process. This is an example of a sin that is both external and internal; where people inwardly follow the influence of *shayṭān* and outwardly disobey the command of Allah.

Not only does Allah allow for devils to oppose Prophets, but He also allows for leaders to emerge among the disbelievers. Leaders who become chief architects of deception which, unbeknownst to them, is ultimately self-deception that will lead them all to Hell.

ĀYĀT 133-147

In this section, Allah demonstrates how different religions were undermined by their people while they followed what was in line with their own desires. They arbitrarily forbade the consumption of certain crops and animals as a means of controlling who was allowed to acquire what. They even killed their own children, under the false assumption that it would be beneficial.

In the end, Allah is the One who created these crops and animals, and therefore, He provides us with the correct instructions on how to handle and use them for their true purpose. Since all of these man-made laws forbidding certain animals have no basis in Divine law, one must question: where did the lawgivers attain the authority through which they place such restrictions?

Allah instructs the Prophet to respond by listing only that which Allah made forbidden for Muslims, together with the more restrictive rules Allah made for the Children of Israel owing to their own transgressions against Allah.

ĀYĀT 148-153

Now Allah directs our attention to who rightfully has authority to determine what is permissible and what is forbidden. In justifying their authority to forbid certain animals, the idolaters put the blame on Allah, saying that He would have stopped them from doing it if He truly did not approve. However, they have no legitimate witnesses or evidence to prove this claim.

Due to this widespread delusion, Allah leaves no doubt regarding what He expects from us, so that our laws and morals are not established based on assumptions. He instructs the Prophet to teach the basic commandments that Allah gives, such as:

- Worshipping One Lord.
- Respecting one's parents.

- Not killing infants and children.
- Avoiding major sins.
- Only killing a life that Allah permits to be killed.
- Protecting orphans.
- Being ethical in business dealings.
- Standing for justice (especially where there is a conflict of interest).
- Keeping one's word.

ĀYĀT 154-165

At the end of this surah, Allah compares the guidance given to the Prophet Muhammad ﷺ with that which was given to Mūsā, showing that anyone who believed in the Torah should have no problem believing in the Qur'an. He then recounts various different excuses that the Children of Israel made for not following the Qur'an; none of which legitimately addresses the fact that the Qur'an contains the truth.

Allah then goes on to explain the contrast between those who seek to violate the religion and the people who follow the straight path. He teaches the Prophet to disassociate with the former, while educating him on how to follow the straight path through the universal legacy of Ibrāhīm; an approach that transcends the specific legacies of the Children of Israel and the Christians. Following this straight path entails dedicating everything in one's life to the will and law of Allah, accepting the human role of stewardship and the Divinely determined hierarchy of Prophethood set by Him. Overall, this implies that all communities of faith should fall under the banner of Prophet Muhammad ﷺ to fulfil their purpose as vicegerents in this world.

SURAH AL-AʿRĀF

ĀYĀT
1-10

Given that the signs and arguments relating to the authority and the power of Allah were detailed in Surah *al-Anʿām*, we will now learn more about the struggle faced by Prophet Muhammad ﷺ to convince his people of this truth.

In this surah, Allah consoles the Prophet, telling him not to be broken by the fanatical rejection by his people, and to stay on course. Allah reassures him that this is not the first time that a Prophet was rejected by his people, and that no matter how severe matters become for believers in this world, justice will be delivered in the next world. Therefore, so long as the Prophet exercises due diligence in spreading the message, the full blame on the Day of Judgment will rest on those who reject him. Moreover, they will have no response to the punishment other than remorse.

Such a position is not surprising, since it was Allah who created us in the first place and gave us everything we have. He has given us full reign to do what we want in this life. Accordingly, it is only just that Allah rewards us for what we have done; whether good or bad.

ĀYĀT
11-20

To gain a comprehensive understanding of how humanity came to disbelieve and argue against guidance, we must start from the beginning with the account of Ādam and Iblīs.

Allah begins the story by explaining that Iblīs was an enemy of humanity even before Ādam and Ḥawwāʾ entered the garden. Allah shows us that he committed the very first sins, specifically the sins of arrogance and racism. Allah educates us on Iblīs's strategy: he will come at humanity from every angle to misguide them. But Allah has given them the knowledge required to handle this test and persevere. Thus, those who choose to follow Iblīs, will follow him not due to a lack of knowledge, but rather a lack of humility with Allah. Consequently, such individuals will be deserving of whatever punishment they bring upon themselves.

As the story unfolds, we learn that Iblīs uses deception to convince Ādam and Ḥawwā' to disobey their Lord. He encourages them to give preference to their desires over their knowledge, thereby exposing their weaknesses. However, due to the knowledge Allah gave them, they were able to recover and repent to Allah, whereas Iblīs persisted in wrongdoing and did not repent.

Allah draws parallels between this story and the guidance given to humanity, since we are all children of Ādam and share his struggles. Allah has given us clothing to cover our weakness, just as He gave Ādam and Ḥawwā'. But He advises us to avoid being allured to disobedience by the devil in the way that they were. He also teaches us not to try to justify our sins like the devil did. Rather, we must stand for justice, worship, and show humility to Allah, thereby, distinguishing ourselves as those who follow Allah and not those who follow the devil.

ĀYĀT 21-42

Another evil humanity has fallen into is forbidding things that Allah has not made forbidden. He has given us clothing, food, and drink for our own benefit so that we can properly worship Him, and He only forbade that which He knows is harmful to us in this life and the next. Therefore, we must follow the Messengers He has sent to us for our own good and avoid making up lies about Allah, His guidance, and His Messengers, lest we meet the Angel of Death in a state of disobedience. If that were to occur, we would surely suffer the consequences of our arrogance.

Allah then provides vivid detail of what those consequences look like; with disbelievers entering into Hell in droves, cursing and blaming each other only to find their punishments increased. Allah further explains how they will be completely encompassed in fire, unable to escape.

In contrast, the believers will have the full bliss of residing in Paradise, grateful that they followed their Messengers and that they accepted guidance.

In this section, Allah presents us with the dialogue between those in Heaven and those in Hell. He shows that each group received exactly what Allah had promised them based on their choices.

Those who have not entered either of those places will observe the contrast between them. As these verses serve as reminder that, as long as we are alive, we should study the promises of Allah and live our lives according to the type of Hereafter we would like to experience. Those who lie about Allah, are arrogant, prideful, toy with the religion, and are deluded by the world will be the most despised and tormented on the Day of Judgment. Meanwhile, those who are humble, religious, and who follow the guidance of the Messengers will be the most envied on that day.

Allah has bestowed upon us a Book that details everything we need to know to succeed in the Hereafter. In it, He reminds us that all things in the heavens and the earth already submit to His will, and that we are asked to do so out of love instead of force. We should spend our time worshipping him and refrain from spreading corruption in this world that He has given us.

Now that the stage has been set, regarding the principles and outcome of disobedience and obedience, Allah starts to provide us with examples of how various generations after Ādam argued with their Prophets.

> Allah educates us on Iblīs's strategy: he will come at humanity from every angle to misguide them. But Allah has given them the knowledge required to handle this test and persevere.

He starts by using the analogy that we can all witness in nature; how He brings rain (guidance) to different lands (hearts) but the results depend on how good or bad the land is, and it simply reflects what lies underneath it.

Allah first introduces Nūḥ and his people. He relays to us that Nūḥ came to them as a brother, to direct them to the truth. He sought to advise them in following the guidance of Allah; a guidance they had neglected since the time of Ādam. But the majority rejected him and continued following their leaders and worshipping idols. Consequently, those who rejected him were punished while those who followed him were saved.

Likewise, Allah sent Prophet Hūd to his people, and they recalled what had happened to the people of Nūḥ some generations before them. Yet, they rejected the advice of their Prophet, instead deciding to follow their leaders and worship other than Allah. They too were destroyed, while the believers were saved.

Allah subsequently relays the story of Ṣāliḥ, and his struggle to convince his people to follow the guidance of Allah. They too recalled what had happened to the people before them in recent history. This time, the people were given an independent sign validating the claims of their Prophet. Nevertheless, consistent with the pattern of previous generations, they followed their leaders and rejected him due to their arrogance. They killed the camel that was sent as a sign for them to believe. Once again, Allah destroyed them and saved the believers.

In the case of Lūṭ, he was sent to his people, imploring them to abandon practices of homosexuality and sodomy. On this occasion, the disbelievers decided to banish their Prophet. So Allah destroyed them and saved the believers.

The last story Allah presents to us in this section is that of Shu'ayb.

He outlines how he was sent to guide his people to Allah and to direct them from their fraudulent business practices. As we learn in the next Juz, they too would suffer the same fate as their predecessors who rejected their Prophets.

This is why Allah reminds the Prophet that all he must do is relay the message and allow people to believe or reject it. In the end, Allah will judge everyone just as He judged those before us, and there will be no difference in the outcome.

PERSONAL REFLECTIONS

Juz 9

TRUE LIBERATION

ĀYĀT 88-102

Concluding the story of Prophet Shuʻayb, Allah shows us how his community followed the same pattern of disbelief that we saw in other stories. They blindly followed their leaders, threatened to banish Prophet Shuʻayb and his followers, and ultimately suffered a great punishment like their predecessors.

Hence, Allah teaches us a fundamental lesson from history: that the Divine justice of Allah is inevitable. There is no escape from Divine accountability, which will either begin in this life or in the next. Thus, no society should become complacent with the blessings of Allah, lest they are punished and replaced due to their ingratitude.

It is precisely for this reason that Allah sends Messengers to humankind. The Messengers are tasked with guiding people away from their own corruption and saving them from the consequences of their sins, before a Divine intervention is called for. Nevertheless, historically we find that humanity turns their backs on the covenants that Allah gives them. Instead, they choose to challenge the power of Allah and to persist in their corruption.

ĀYĀT 103-131

Here Allah brings us the primary example of the struggle between truth and falsehood: Mūsā and the Pharaoh.

Allah does not start by relaying details of the childhood of Prophet Mūsā. Rather, He describes the beginning of the Prophetic mission undertaken by Mūsā, since this is directly related to the theme of the surah. Here we receive a detailed account of the clear miracles Mūsā delivered to the Pharaoh. Yet, we find that the Pharaoh rejected the obvious truth and falsely accused Mūsā of working magic. We also are informed of how the Pharaoh used his position to sway his people and influence public opinion about the Prophet, despite the many weaknesses in his arguments. He was so arrogant and confident in his disbelief that he even held a public event dedicated to "exposing" the "magic" of Mūsā by testing him against real magicians.

Even so, we find that all his tactics were turned against him. Not only were the magicians defeated, but they publicly submitted to Allah. Despite all of his plans being exposed, we find the Pharaoh making up a new claim to absolve himself from the responsibility of accepting the truth. The Pharaoh concludes that the magicians must have colluded with Mūsā beforehand, and through this claim he continues to influence the public towards siding with him.

At this point, Allah introduces us to the second stage of this struggle between belief and disbelief. At first, the Pharaoh invited Mūsā to prove his Prophethood. Now, in these *āyāt* we see that the Pharaoh makes it clear that no miracle will ever convince him. We notice that he has attained a greater state of disbelief than he had previously publicized. Even the followers of Mūsā were starting to be influenced by this thinking. They began to blame Mūsā for any problem they would suffer, thereby laying the foundation for the type of insolence they would display after this stage was over.

Just to demonstrate how backwards the Pharaoh and his people's disbelief was, Allah tells us about the various afflictions he placed on their society. Every time they were overwhelmed with a supernatural tragedy, they would ask Mūsā to pray to Allah to save them and insist that this would convince them to believe in Him. These tragedies happened repeatedly, yet every time his prayer was answered they would still refuse to submit to Allah. At this point, there was no excuse remaining for anyone to disbelieve in Prophet Mūsā.

Ultimately, the Pharaoh and those who followed him were destroyed just as the disbelieving societies before them. They were provided every proof and numerous chances to cease their corruption, oppression, and disbelief, but they opted for the punishment instead. Allah replaced them with those who were oppressed. This is the pattern that Allah has established throughout human history.

Unlike the other Prophetic stories mentioned previously, the story of Mūsā is unique. Usually Allah ends the story of a Prophet by stating how he and his followers were saved. Yet here, the story is exceptionally different because Allah provides a glimpse into what happened after the followers of the Prophet Mūsā were saved, and how many of them, too, eventually returned to misguidance. This could be considered the third stage of the struggle between belief and disbelief: avoiding new forms of polytheism.

Interestingly, this stage is where the story of the Children of Israel began in Surah *al-Baqarah*; after they were saved from the Pharaoh. Part of the reason for this is that in Surah *al-Baqarah*, Allah was addressing the Children of Israel by giving them the proofs they needed to accept Prophet Muhammad ﷺ by reminding them of their previous actions. On the other hand, Surah *al-Anfāl* is addressing Prophet Muhammad ﷺ and comparing the general conflict of truth and falsehood. Since there is no greater historical advocate of falsehood than the Pharaoh, it is befitting to start the story by introducing him. That said, the struggle does not end there; it continues with the internal struggle between truth and falsehood *within* the community of faith. Hence, there are further details that are worthy of mention from the time after the Exodus. These events are relevant to the believers, as they would teach them how to avoid repeating the same mistakes of the communities that were saved before them but then deviated away from guidance and were influenced into becoming tyrants themselves.

One of the new details highlighted is the account of Mūsā asking to see Allah after his forty night isolation in worship, only to return to his people – revelations in hand – to find them worshipping a calf. They even threatened the life of Prophet Hārūn if he were to oppose them. Here we learn that even though a person might be physically saved by following a Prophet in form, they will always be prone to misguidance if they never accept their Prophet in spirit. Consequently, as soon as an opportunity presents itself through which they find comfort, they will cease it, even if it entails disbelief. Moreover, these people will face their punishment in the Hereafter even though they do not suffer the same fate as the disbelievers in this world. There is a silver lining, however, because Allah shows that there is still opportunity for these types of people to repent, even after they corrupted their religion and fell into misguidance.

ĀYĀT 156-178

In this section, Allah introduces the fourth stage of disbelief in this story; ingratitude with blessings. Before describing this stage, He highlights the ways in which Prophet Muhammad ﷺ is similar to Prophet Mūsā. He too will liberate the people from the shackles of oppression and will lift the burdens of sin and ignorance through his guidance. Moreover, he too will lead humanity to the salvation, forgiveness, and mercy of Allah. Unlike the time of Prophet Mūsā, however, these benefits will not be exclusive to the Children of Israel; rather, they will be for humanity as a whole.

From there, Allah continues by showing us the numerous miraculous blessings He bestowed upon the Children of Israel: He made each tribe into a nation, produced water from stone, sent down manna and quails, and liberated land for them, among other things. Yet, even after all these blessings, many of them showed ingratitude, and the prime example of this is their violation of the

Sabbath; a violation that continues till today. Each time they violated their blessings, Allah would send a punishment or trial to return them to guidance. The cycle would continue repeatedly for generations. Some of them would learn the lesson and follow the truth, while others would not; instead, accepting falsehood for material gain while taking it for granted that they will be forgiven.

At this point it becomes clear that no matter what sign or punishment is given, some people will not accept guidance. Even if a mountain were suspended above their heads. They will continue to claim they are following their forefathers, regardless of how ignorant the latter's practices were.

In case one thought that this disbelief was due to a lack of knowledge, Allah reminds us of the story of Bal'am who had an immense amount of knowledge, but he preferred to follow his desires over guidance and went astray. In sum, only those who turn to Allah for guidance will be guided by Him, and whoever submits to misguidance will suffer nothing but loss.

ĀYĀT
179-206

Now that Allah has shed light on the struggles of previous Prophets and the lessons we can take from them, He once again directs our focus to the Prophet Muhammad ﷺ and the trials of this age of Islam. Essentially, Allah has given humanity the ability to choose, and with that comes the ability to be rewarded or punished. It is this concept that humans recognise to be true. The signs of the presence of Allah are everywhere. Nevertheless, there are those who decide to close off their senses from receiving guidance and from the people who accept and follow it. Therefore, we should not be surprised if Allah allows disbelievers to enjoy the comforts of this world because we know that this is temporary and that justice will eventually be served. What is important is to realize that this justice is in accordance with His timing, not ours.

Ending the surah, Allah lays out why it is counterintuitive to worship anyone other than Him. He reminds us that He is the one who created mankind, starting from a single soul, and allowed it to flourish. It was only after Ādam and Ḥawwā' had children, by His permission, that men and women began to associate partners with Him.

He reminds us that these false deities have no power of their own, and He is the ultimate provider of any sense of security and the only One who can respond to us if we seek aid.

He instructs the Prophet to continue his worship and continue on his path of encouraging good. In the end, he will find those who will seek guidance from the Qur'an and who will worship Allah alongside him. Others will wilfully fall under the devil's misguidance and try to oppose His plan. Unfortunately for them, His plan never fails.

SURAH AL-ANFĀL

ĀYĀT
1-19

In the previous surah, Allah placed much emphasis on the struggles the Prophets experienced at the hands of the disbelieving communities throughout history. Now, in Surah *al-Anfāl*, Allah shifts the discussion to address the believers around Prophet Muhammad ﷺ and gives them the guidance they need to overcome adversity and gain their rewards. Unlike the Prophets of the past, Prophet Muhammad ﷺ will actually defeat his enemies without them being completely destroyed by Allah.

Allah starts by giving descriptions of who the true believers are and what their hearts are attached to. He continues by showing us how they prayed to Him and He aided them by giving them victory internally and externally in the Battle of Badr, while He made the disbelievers taste defeat.

Allah leaves no room for believers to rout and retreat on the battlefield since He has promised that He will bring victory. They must understand that ultimately, there is no one that can grant them victory except Allah. Moreover, this battle teaches them that they are simply tasked with doing the work required of them and then watching Allah bring forth the results. Hence, the only obligation they need to fulfil to be successful is to obey Allah and His Messenger.

In contrast to those who obey the Messenger, Allah describes the people who are close-minded and forget the blessings that come with the guidance delivered by the Prophet. This disobedience does not only affect that one individual, but the entire community. Allah reminds us that there was once a time when anyone could have attacked the believers in their most vulnerable state. Thus, they must not become deluded by the victories or wealth that they attain. All they earn is from Allah alone, and He is the One protecting the believers and using them as means to defeat the disbelievers.

Allah shows us how His plan entails the self-destruction of the enemies of the Prophet rather than a supernatural punishment, as was sent upon the past communities. This allows time for the good people among them to emerge and for the sinners to have the opportunity of returning to Allah. Hence, Allah instructs the Prophet to fight against religious oppression for His sake, and to know that regardless of what the enemies do, Allah will always be his Protector.

PERSONAL REFLECTIONS

Juz 10

HYPOCRISY

ĀYĀT 41-54

Now that Allah has explained the reality of victory in the previous surah, He draws our attention to the different perspectives of battle.

He starts with the believers, and how He favours them with the ability to see the enemy as if they were smaller and weaker than they present themselves to be. Through this, the believers gain greater confidence in their own abilities and are less fearful of the enemies' capabilities. This sense of comfort Allah provides to the believers is essential in giving them the courage to move forward. All they now have to do is simply continue to obey Allah and His Messenger and avoid infighting.

On the other hand, the disbelievers have a perspective that is grounded in conceitedness and relies heavily on the schemes of devils. Instead of realizing their plot, they will see the angels tormenting them on the battlefield.

Allah reminds us that this is the same pattern observed with the people of the Pharaoh – as discussed in the previous Juz.

ĀYĀT 55-66

After giving us an insight into the contrasting perspectives, Allah addresses how those perspectives affect the alliances. Certain individuals seek peace, and such people should be our allies. However, there are also those who openly break their alliances, and others who are secretly treacherous. Allah instructs the believers that they should always be prepared to defend the community from such individuals, thereby ensuring that they are proactively showcasing their abilities to deter any aggression.

As for the believers, they will be the people who can be relied on for support. Their faith unites them and gives them fortitude to con-

> Believers are obligated to support and defend one another, just as the enemies support and defend each other. Consequently, the believers' survival depends on them uniting.

front their enemies. Hence, Allah regulates what would be considered reasonable odds for a believer to stand his ground and what are unreasonable, depending on their strength at the time.

Up to this point in the surah, Allah has elaborated on the nature of spoils, treachery, victory and defeat, as well as the dichotomy of war and peace. He has also given us tangible examples of how this plays out in the battlefield. Now, as the surah comes to a close, Allah concludes by guiding us on how we must take responsibility for preserving human life, especially during times of war.

First, Allah singles out the subject of captives of war, reiterating that they still have an opportunity to repent and seek forgiveness. Furthermore, Allah instructs us not to worry about the treachery of the prisoners of war: Allah defeated them before, and He will defeat them again.

As for the responsibility that the believers have towards one another, this is laid out in detail. Believers are obligated to support and defend one another, just as the enemies support and defend each other. Consequently, the believers' survival depends on them uniting.

In terms of who is most deserving of support, Allah lists the Migrants (Muhājirūn), the Supporters (Anṣār), and the hierarchy of blood relatives.

Through this surah, Allah provides the believers with a comprehensive understanding of how Allah will hold them accountable, and how they should hold themselves accountable. Thus, this surah aligns their priorities according to what Allah wants, as opposed to their desires.

SURAH AL-TAWBAH

ĀYĀT 1-15

In the last surah, Allah clarified the lessons that believers needed to learn from the battles they had engaged in since their migration to Madinah. The rules concerning the spoils of war, allies and foes, treachery, preparations, and odds have all been explained. By the time we reach this surah, we are in a good position to learn how Allah wants us to operate in the event that a treaty is breached in its entirety. Thus, this surah opens with the theme of war against those who have violated the Treaty of Ḥudaybiyah, and by extension, signals the beginning of the Conquest of Makkah.

Once again, Allah reminds us that repentance is always an option for those who wish to change their ways and embrace Islam. As for those who broke the treaty, they have made themselves open enemies of the believers. The only alternative option before them is to seek protection with the Muslims.

Such an option is fair as the Muslims and their allies were the party that maintained the treaty, while the disbelievers and Quraysh broke the treaty making them the aggressors. At this point, after over twenty years of slander, thievery, assassinations, lynching, and religious suppression from the idolatrous Quraysh, it was time to end their reign and permanently reinstate the religion of Ibrāhīm (Islam) to its rightful place; in Makkah. The Arabian Peninsula was finally ready for this event, and here Allah explains the strategic and political reasons why it was so imperative.

ĀYĀT 16-37

Now that the political ties have been severed and the strategic reasoning for this conquest has been laid down, Allah shifts the focus to the moral and religious right of the Prophet to establish Islam in Makkah.

Makkah was founded and established on Islam and monotheistic belief. Moreover, it was managed by the direct descendants of Ibrāhīm, who was the historical champion of Islam and monotheism. Therefore, it makes no sense for Makkah to continue to be led by idol worshippers who undermined the religion of Ibrāhīm. Even if the people of Quraysh upheld the caretaking of the Kaaba and hosted the pilgrims for the hajj, their entire religious culture was based on idolatry. Accordingly, they did not deserve the privilege of maintaining those roles so long as they were undertaking them for idolatrous reasons. This is especially true now that a rightful Prophetic heir to Prophet Ibrāhīm exists among them and has re-established the religion of Ibrāhīm.

Furthermore, Allah emphasizes that the moral authority of the Prophet overrides our relationships with our family, tribe, wealth, or business. His authority was given to him by Allah, which makes our relationship with Allah contingent on our relationship with him, and our success from Allah dependent on our allegiance to him.

Consequently, Allah tasks the believers with removing the idolaters from the Sacred Grounds – regardless of their ties of kinship or business – on the basis that they have broken the treaty and have defiled the Kaaba with idolatry. The Children of Israel and the Christians fall into the same category as they, too, have defiled their Prophetic religions with forms of idolatry.

Allah establishes the truth of the religions of the past by exposing the deviances that have become commonplace: worshiping saints, usurping and hoarding of wealth without giving charity, and tampering with time and the calendar resulting in the creation of leap days, months, and even years. All of this further emphasizes the authority of Prophet Muhammad ﷺ over us in establishing the correct religion of Allah.

ĀYĀT 38-66

Now that the idolaters, Children of Israel, and Christians have been addressed, Allah directs our attention to the hypocrites. The hypocrites are outwardly Muslim, thereby, ensuring they cannot be banished from the Sacred Grounds. Additionally, they have not declared war and thus do not deserve to be fought. Therefore, Allah exposes their practices so that their influence can be minimized and the trials they subject the believers to are recognized.

Here Allah lists a number of their traits, including the following:

1. They always lag behind when ordered to fight in battles with the Prophet. Yet, Allah reminds them that He does not need them to give victory to His Prophet; just as they were not needed when he and Abū Bakr were in the cave during the migration. Ultimately, fighting for the sake of Allah is for their benefit, not for the benefit of Allah or His Messenger.

2. They make up excuses and lies for not upholding their obligation to fight in battle. Here Allah reminds us that they are a liability to the believers and that they would intentionally cause more harm than good.

3. They look forward to seeing the believers suffering and hate to see them succeed.

4. Their charitable efforts are not accepted because of their insincere intentions and because they do not ground themselves in prayer and worship.

5. They lie and swear by Allah to convince people they are telling the truth instead of relying on their actions to prove it.

6. They are greedy for wealth even when they do not need it.

7. They mock the Prophet and call him names.

8. They joke about sacred matters.

ĀYĀT 67-74

At this point of the surah, Allah draws our focus to a particular practice of hypocrisy that is very distinct from the practice of the believers. He says that they encourage and accommodate sin while discouraging good deeds. In contrast, the believers protect each other by discouraging sin and encouraging good deeds.

It is this stark difference that stands out in each story in history. Those who were destroyed in the past displayed the same hypocritical trait, while the Prophets and the believers consistently upheld the Divine standard of guidance.

Allah reminds the Prophet to continue to struggle with them and with the disbelievers, as this is part of the natural process that comes with the responsibility of upholding the religion.

ĀYĀT 75-92

At the close of this Juz, Allah highlights the two major factors that contribute to hypocrisy. In both cases we are taught that, irrespective of the oaths that are made and assurances that are given, the hypocrites will find ways to avoid fulfilling these obligations.

The first of these factors is not giving wealth for the sake of Allah and ill treatment of the poor. The hypocrites value wealth to such an extent that they will do anything to gain it, and once they have it, they will be stingy with it. Moreover, they mock those who do not have it due to their assumption that it has an inherent value.

The second main factor causing hypocrisy is cowardice when it comes to fighting for the sake of Allah. They are not just so afraid of fighting that they remain behind; rather, they enjoy going against their obligations.

Such lack of action was often observed among the hypocrites, especially in battles that required great sacrifice and where the odds were, at face value, not in their favour. Yet, when the odds seemed to be in their favour or they believed that they would reap a great amount of spoils, they would try to participate just enough that they could gain the worldly benefits while still minimizing their individual risk.

Allah emphasizes that these are people who will not be forgiven for their betrayal. Moreover, their worldly possessions will prove to be a hardship for them instead of a blessing.

That said, Allah exempts those with legitimate reasons to stay behind by stating that, although they cannot go out to fight, their hearts are in the right place. It is clear that in staying behind, such individuals are full of remorse for not being able to contribute to the cause. These people will gain the reward of Allah because He knows what is in their hearts.

PERSONAL REFLECTIONS

ABOUT THE AUTHOR

Imam Hamzah Abdul-Malik is a Hafiz of Qur'an who holds a bachelors in Islamic Law and a masters in Islamic Leadership. He traveled the world to study with traditional scholars and has over 15 years of formal traditional Islamic education from Jami' Imam an-Nafi' in Morocco, Abu Noor in Damascus, Dar al-Mustapha in Tarim, and al-Azhar University. In 2012, he returned home to the states to raise his family and invest his knowledge and training into community building and Islamic education. He founded Midtown Mosque and Miraaj Academy and hopes to bring all of his experiences and skills together to serve the Muslim community.

www.ingramcontent.com/pod-product-compliance
Lightning Source LLC
Chambersburg PA
CBHW030451010526
44118CB00011B/885